LAUGH YOUR
SOCKS OFF!

WORLD'S BEST
(AND WORST)
CREEPY CRITTER JOKES

JESSICA RUSICK

Lerner Publications ◆ Minneapolis

>>>>>>>>>>>>>>>>>>>>>>>>>

Q Why was the slug late for work?

A He lost track of slime.

Lerner Publications Company
An imprint of Lerner Publishing Group, Inc.
241 First Avenue North
Minneapolis, MN 55401 USA

For reading levels and more information, look up this title at www.lernerbooks.com.

Main body text set in Billy Infant Regular.
Typeface provided by SparkyType.

Library of Congress Cataloging-in-Publication Data

Names: Rusick, Jessica, author.
Title: World's best (and worst) creepy critter jokes / Jessica Rusick.
Description: Minneapolis : Lerner Publications, [2020] | Series: Laugh your socks off! | Audience: Ages: 6-10. | Audience: Grades: K-3. | Summary: "How do fleas travel? And what is a mouse's favorite game? These jokes are perfect for bugging your friends, and some will even have you groaning and laughing at the same time"— Provided by publisher.
Identifiers: LCCN 2019018530 (print) | LCCN 2019980723 (ebook) | ISBN 9781541576957 (library binding) | ISBN 9781541589063 (paperback) | ISBN 9781541583153 (pdf)
Subjects: LCSH: Animals—Juvenile humor. | Wit and humor, Juvenile.
Classification: LCC PN6231.A5 R87 2020 (print) | LCC PN6231.A5 (ebook) | DDC 818/.602080362—dc23

LC record available at https://lccn.loc.gov/2019018530
LC ebook record available at https://lccn.loc.gov/2019980723

Manufactured in the United States of America
1 - CG - 12/31/19

Knock, knock. Who's there?
Worm. Worm who?
Worm me up, I'm freezing!

Q What happened to the snail who lost his shell?

A He felt sluggish.

>>>>>>>>>>>>>>>>>>>>>>>>>>>>>>>>>>

Q What lies on the ground, one hundred feet in the air?

A A centipede lying on its back.

<<<<<<<<<<<<<<<<<<<<<<

Q Why do worms like to sleep in?

A Because the early bird catches the worm.

KNEE-SLAPPER

Q What did the slug do after he won the lottery?

A He bought a snail-boat!

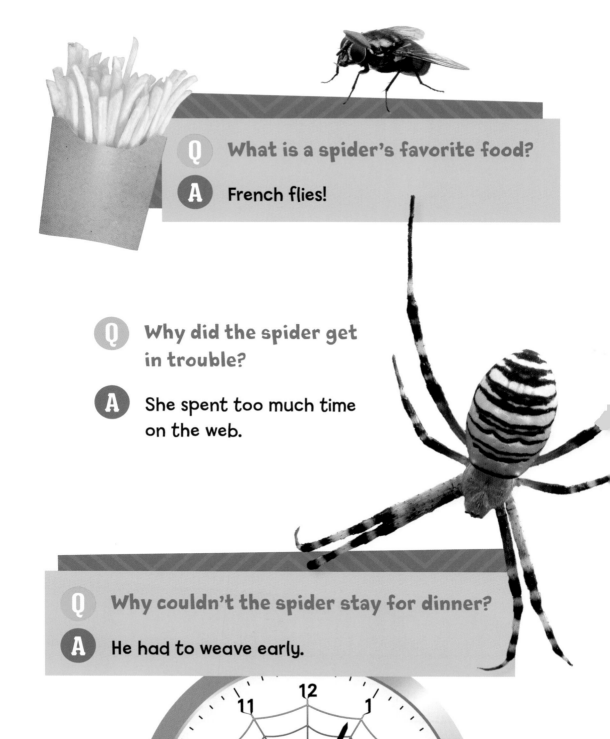

Q What is a spider's favorite food?

A French flies!

Q Why did the spider get in trouble?

A She spent too much time on the web.

Q Why couldn't the spider stay for dinner?

A He had to weave early.

Q What do you get when you cross a spider with an ear of corn?

A A cobweb!

Q What did the spider do when she got her new bike?

A She took it for a spin.

Q What is a mouse's favorite game?

A Hide and squeak!

HA! HA!

Q What do you get when you cross a mouse with a freezer?

A A mice cube.

6

Q Why did the mouse stay indoors?

A Because it was raining cats and dogs.

\>>>>>>>>>>>>>>>>>>>>>>>>>>>>>

Q What do you call a mole who prays?

A A holy moly!

<<<<<<<<<<<<<<<<<<<<<<<<<<

Q What's black and white and black and white and yellow?

A Two skunks fighting over a banana.

Q Did you hear about the skunk who wrote a book?

A It was a best-smeller!

GROANER AWARD

Q Why did the mole do well on the test?

A Because it was mole-tiple choice.

A toad and a duck were sitting by a pond talking. Time flies when you're having fun, the duck said.

That's not right, the toad said.

TIME IS FUN WHEN YOU'RE HAVING FLIES!

Q Where do frogs hang out in the summer?

A At the tad pool.

Q Why was the frog cold?

A She was sitting on a chilly pad!

Q Where do fancy frogs go for fun?

A To the hop-era!

Q What did the toad say when he saw his friend?

A Wart's up?

KNEE-SLAPPER

Q What did the frog say when the librarian brought her a book?

A She had already read it, read it, read it.

Baby Bat: Mom, can I have a bicycle?

Mama Bat: I don't know. That sounds like a wheely bat idea.

Knock, knock. Who's there?
Bat. Bat who?
Bat you'll never guess who's knocking!

Q Why are bats the best dinner guests?

A They always give fangs for their meals.

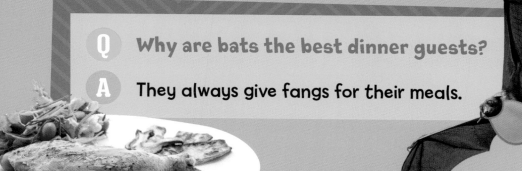

Q What do bats do on the weekends?

A They just hang around.

Q Why couldn't the mosquito fall asleep?

A She kept having bite-mares.

Q Where do bees wait for the bus?

A At the buzz stop!

Q Why did the bee go to the doctor?

A Because she had hives.

Q Why did the fly stay home?

A He had the flew.

GROANER AWARD

Q How do bees brush their hair?

A With honeycombs.

A police officer sees a man driving around with a car full of lizards.

You better take them to the zoo right now, the officer tells the man. The man says he will.

The next day, the police officer sees the man is still driving around with the lizards. Now, the lizards are wearing sunglasses.

I thought I told you to take these lizards to the zoo, the police officer says.

I did, the man says.

AND TODAY I'M TAKING THEM TO THE BEACH!

14

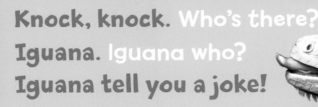

Knock, knock. Who's there?
Iguana. Iguana who?
Iguana tell you a joke!

HA! HA!

Q What do you get when you cross a gecko and a snowstorm?

A A blizzard.

Larry Lizard didn't want to take a bath. Get in the tub, Larry, his mother said. You skink!

Q What's worse than finding an alligator in your bedroom?

A Finding two alligators in your bedroom.

Q What do you get when you cross a kangaroo with a snake?

A A jump rope!

Q What is a snake's favorite dance?

A The mamba.

Q What happened to the snake who sneezed?

A She had to viper nose.

Q How do you keep a baby snake happy?

A Give it a rattle.

GROANER AWARD

Q Which snake is the best baker?

A A pie-thon!

17

Q What did the great squid thinker say?

A I ink, therefore I am.

Q What happened when the squid saw a red light?

A He squid-ed to a stop.

Q Why can't jellyfish tell good jokes?

A They don't have a funny bone in their bodies.

Q What is a jellyfish's favorite food?

A Sting cheese.

Q How do fleas travel?

A They itch-hike!

Q Why didn't the termite go see the movie?

A She liked the book better.

I saw a great bug magician last night. He did a ton of magic ticks!

KNEE-SLAPPER

Q What do you call a bedbug police officer?

A An undercover cop.

HA!

Q What do pests use to mine for gold?

A DynaMITE.

Q What is a pest's favorite dessert?

A Lice cream!

Q What is a crab's favorite fruit?

A A crabapple.

Q Why did the lobster go to jail?

A He broke the claw.

Q What do you call a lobster on a baseball field?

A The pincher.

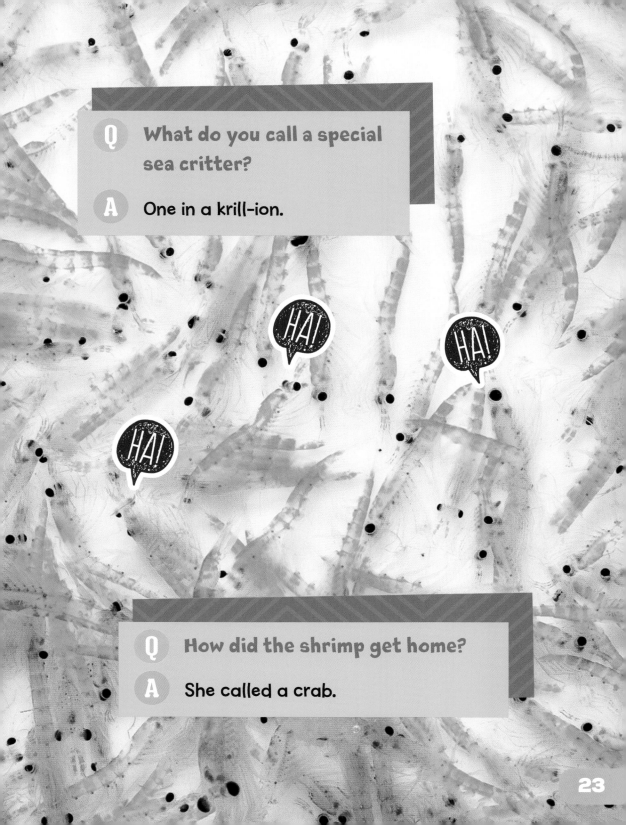

Q What do you call a special sea critter?

A One in a krill-ion.

Q How did the shrimp get home?

A She called a crab.

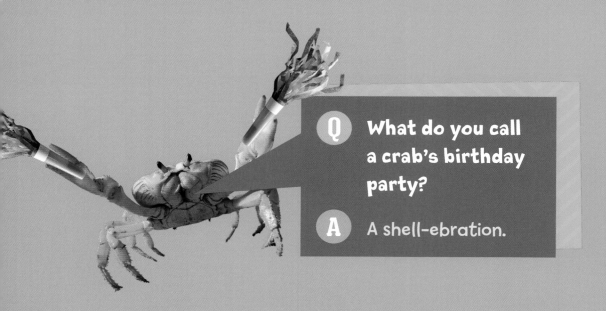

Q What do you call a crab's birthday party?

A A shell-ebration.